PRACTICAL HOMŒOPATHY, FOR THE PEOPLE,

ADAPTED TO THE COMPREHENSION OF THE NON-PROFESSIONAL,

AND FOR

Reference by the Young Practitioner,

INCLUDING A NUMBER OF MOST

VALUABLE NEW REMEDIES AND IMPROVEMENTS IN THE TREATMENT OF NUMEROUS DISEASES NOT IN GENERAL USE.

SECOND EDITION.

BY J. S. DOUGLAS, A. M., M. D.,

Late Professor of Mat. Med., Special Pathology and Diagnosis in the Western Hom. Med. College at Cleaveland, Ohio Fellow and Corresponding Member of the Penn. Hom. Medicai College at Philadelphia. Author of "Treatment of Intermittent Fevers." "Homœopathy, its Princple and Practice Explained, and Illustrated," &c.

MILWAUKEE:
1862.

STEREOTYPED BY SIAS & HILL,
NORTH-WESTERN TYPE FOUNDRY, MILWAUKEE.

PREFACE.

In furnishing the public with Homœopathic remedies, with directions for their use, it is proper to state the motives for so doing. These are—

FIRST.—A knowledge of the vast superiority of Homœopathic treatment, over the old system.

SECOND.—A large portion of the population, of the West especially, are not within reach of a Homœopothic physician, and if they employ the remedies, are obliged to depend upon such knowledge of them as they can acquire from books, designed for domestic use.

THIRD.—Though there have been many works published for this purpose, they are so large and obscure, that they perplex and confound, rather than instruct and guide, those not accustomed to medical studies. The constant call is for something short and plain.

FOURTH.—These large works are years behind the actual knowledge of the present day, in regard to medicines and the treatment of the most common diseases. A work is needed, corresponding to the present advanced state of medical knowledge.

There will be found in this little work a considerable number of the most important remedies, not mentioned in any of these large works, and new and important applications of several others.

FIFTH.—The reputation of Homœopathic remedies has become so general, and the demand for them so great that the country is becoming flooded with Homœopathic quackery, under the name of "Specific Homœopathic Remedies," no one knowing what they are but him who prepares them. When a bottle or box is exhausted, the owner has no resource but to send to the getter-up of these nostrums, or some of his agents, to get it replenished. The unfortunate example of this mode of quackery has been set by a medical man at the East, who has thereby forfeited his standing in the profession, and been very properly expelled from the American Medical Society. His example is being followed by others who have a higher regard for their own pockets than their professional reputation, or the interest of the public.

All reasoning persons will prefer to know what the medicines are which they use, and when one is exhausted be able to replenish it at any place where Homœopathic medicines are kept, and at the same time enjoy the practical benefits of knowing what the remedies are which effect cures of different diseases.

Besides these considerations, any reasoning person, by a moment's reflection, will be convinced how totally inadequate these "Specifics" are to cure all the diseases for which they are advertised, and how unsafe it must be to trust them. We have no hesitation in saying to the public, that it is totally unsafe to trust to these "Specific Remedies," for the treatment of the various diseases for which they are prescribed, as much so as to trust the thousand other mixtures advertised to cure everything.

The deficiencies and inconveniences of existing domestic works, I propose to remedy, while the quackery is avoided. Those who use the remedies will know what they are using—will rapidly gain a knowledge of their properties and effects, and thus be acquiring valuable medical knowledge.

I do not aim to make accomplished physicians of the public, nor expect that *every* case of disease can be safely treated domestically. But I do know, from numerous examples of domestic practice, that a long catalogue of acute and serious diseases, as well as lighter disorders, will be treated much more safely and successfully by families, by following the directions here given, than they are treated by the best drugging physicians.

Nor it is my design to treat of every disease to which humanity is subject, nor to prescribe every remedy of the Materia Medica. But I shall give brief and unmistakable directions for *curing* the great mass of diseases of the country, constituting nine-tenths of all the cases for which the physician is usually consulted, with remedies enough to meet these cases, among which is a considerable number of most valuable and even indispensable remedies, which are not yet in use even by Homœopathic physicians generally.

It is greatly to be regretted that so many Allopathic physicians are dabbling with Homœopathic remedies, and pretending that they can practice Homœopathy where it is appropriate, as well as we, without any of the study or knowledge necessary to use them with any success or credit to the system. When, by their bungling misapplication of these beautiful remedies, they fail of success, or, by giving them in Allopathic doses, do serious mischief, they pronounce Homœopathy not adapted to such cases. As well might a bungler, after spoiling a board and mangling his hand, by attempting to use a saw, pronounce a saw not adapted to such purposes.

In short, my one great object in this issue of medicines, with appropriate directions, is to make known and extend the blessings of Homœopathic remedies properly applied, by bringing the community to a practical acquaintance with them, and induce them to witness their beneficient effects under their own administration and experience. We hope that very many who have never used Homœopathic remedies will be induced to make the trial.

It will not be deemed egotistic by those who know him, or know of him, to say that this work is written, and the medicines selected and prepared by one who has devoted over thirty years to the *study* as well as the *practice* of medicine, and who, in his intercourse with the best and most progressive physicians of the day, and in the performance of his duties as a teacher of medicine, the reading of the latest practical works, and the habitual proving of new remedies on himself and others, has anxiously labored to collect practical information, and apply it to the treatment of disease.

INTRODUCTION.

Most persons who have not given special attention to Homœopathy, have very mistaken notions of it. It is very commonly thought to consist in giving very small doses. If an Allopathic physician gives very small doses, it is thought that he is almost Homœopathic. This is a great mistake. One may give just as small doses as we do, and yet make no approach to being Homœopathic. Homœopathy consists in treating disease according to a certain fixed law of cure. This law is expressed by the phrase—"LIKE CURES LIKE." The meaning of this phrase is, that a medicine in small doses, will cure a disease, the like of which, the same medicine will produce on a healthy person, if given in large doses. The first inquiry which we make, when called to treat a disease, is, "What medicine will produce a disease like it, in a healthy person, if given in large doses?" When we find such a remedy, we give it with entire confidence of success, if the disease is curable. The correctness of this law, any one can prove on himself. For example, after one has seen fevers cured in a few hours, by Gelseminum, in doses of half or quarter of a drop, let him test the correctness of this law, by taking, when he is well, five or ten drops of the same remedy. If he is at all sensitive, he will find, within five minutes, that his pulse has from ten to fifteen or twenty fewer beats in the minute, than it had before; and he will feel more or less chilly and dull. This will soon be followed by heat, a quick pulse, flushed face, fullness and pain of the head, and, perhaps, pain of the back and limbs. In short, he will feel that he has got a fever. Soon a prickling of the skin is felt, and a sweat breaks out, and after a few hours, he is well again. Now, it is just because Gelseminum *produces* a fever in LARGE doses, that it *cures* a similar fever in SMALL doses. The first dose I ever took of this remedy, when I was in perfect health, I *knew* that it would cure our prevalent fevers, as well as I know it now, after curing hundreds with it, because I knew that the law of "like cures like," was a true and reliable law. This is the law that guides us in all our treatment of disease. Every remedy prescribed in this book, for particular diseases, is prescribed, because it *produces* a similar disease. This is the secret of our great success, in the most formidable and dangerous diseases, a success that often astonishes those who do not understand the secret. Allopathic physicians have no such law to guide them. The only law they have for treating disease is, the "cut and try" law, or the law of experiment, and all their experiments are made upon the sick, and at their expense. Our experiments are made before hand on the healthy, and we enter at once on the *cure* of the sick, while they are *experiment-*

ing upon them. Our's is a certain science—their's is an uncertain art.

It will be readily seen that we cannot safely give large doses. If we did, we should produce the diseases we now cure. The accuracy of this law is proved to a demonstration, and every one may satisfy himself of it, a layman as well as a physican. And if this is a true law, then the practice of Homœpathy is the true practice, and all others are false. A most intelligent clergyman was investigating the truth of this law, and one day called and related the following case : said he, in my young days I was in the habit of drinking wine. I have a most vivid recollection of the bursting head-ache, the parched mouth, the burning thirst, the nausea and the prostration, the morning after a hard night's drinking. I awoke a few mornings since with all these feelings in a most distressing degree, though I had drank nothing. I related my feelings to my wife, saying that I felt exactly as if I had a night's debauch on wine. She laughingly replied that a Homœopathic dose of wine ought to cure me. I thought it a good chance to test the truth of the principle. I took two drops of wine in some water, and the effect was more remarkable than I ever witnessed from a dose of medicine. In five minutes my mouth was moist, my thirst abated, my head-ache vanishing, my strength returning, and in 15 minutes I was perfectly well. Here was a beautiful illustration of the law. A minute dose—2 drops of Wine, cured, in a prompt and truly Homœpathic manner, a formidable train of symptoms.

like those produced by large doses of the same article. This is equally true of all remedies. Tea produces, in those not accustomed to its use, anxiety, trembling, weakness and palpitation of the heart, yet every lady knows that tea, in moderate quantity, is an excellent remedy for those very symptoms. Allopathic medical authorities furnish a thousand examples which prove this very law, though they do not understand it.

Tobacco, according to all Allopathic authorities, both produces and cures giddiness, nausea, trembling and weakness; agaricus produces and cures epilepsy; belladonna both produces and cures delirium and headache; ipecac and antimony produce and cure nausea and vomiting; nitric acid, iodine and mercury produce and cure salivation and ulceration of the mouth. We might fill a volume with similar examples. Large doses produce diseases—small ones cure them. It may seem strange to those who have not looked at the subject, that the same remedy should act in such contrary directions, and produce and cure the same affections. It is, nevertheless, founded on nature and reason, which is more than can be said of most medical doctrines.

As I am desirous that every man and woman, who reads this book, should know more of the philosophy of medicine than Allopathic physicians do, and be able to meet the arguments brought by them against Homœopathy, I propose to explain the philosophy of this Homœopathic law, so that all will understand it.

It is founded upon a law of life—a vital principle

Let us question nature in this, as in all other things. My hands are cold, and I plunge them into cold water, or rub them in snow, and what is the result? In a few minutes, they are glowing with warmth. This is not a freak of nature. Nature has no freaks. Her laws are uniform and universal, and this is an example of one of her laws. Take another example: My hands are hot, and I plunge them into hot water, and after a few minutes exposure to the air, they become cool. Take other and varied examples: I burn my hand; it is hot, red, inflamed and painful. On Allopathic principles, we should apply cold to remove this heat. And what would be the effect? Why, the heat and pain would be relieved for a short time, but the vital principle of re-action is aroused against it, and the hand soon becomes more hot, red, and painful than before. Hence, experience, without a knowledge of the law, has taught the profession, that cold applications to a burn, though a comfortable temporary palliative, is a very bad curative. But adopt an opposite treatment, and apply a heating stimulant, as alcohol, or spirits of turpentine, or soft soap. The vital principle reacts against this, also, and in a short time, the heat, pain and inflammation subside, a comfortable coolness follows, and the burn is soon cured.

A restless patient is put to sleep on opium, but on the following night, he is more restless and sleepless than before. We might give a thousand examples of a similar character.

This will enable us to understand two universal and practical laws, of the action of remedies, which the community should understand, if physicians do not. Such an understanding will do away with an immense amount of all pervading and mischievous quackery.

First Law.—Every medicine produces two directly opposite effects, in the order of time. The first, the primary and transient effect; the second, the secondary and more permanent one.

To illustrate this law by an example: a patient takes a cathartic or a laxative. Its first or primary effect, is, to stimulate the intestines to unusual, unnatural activity; so much so, that he has, during its action, a medicinal diarrhœa. But this effect is transient, lasting only a few hours. Then comes the secondary effect, which is exactly the opposite, viz.: unusual and unnatural inactivity and torpor, producing constipation.

Another illustration: opium or morphine is given to allay pain and procure rest and sleep. This purpose is answered by its primary effect; but this soon ceases, and then comes the opposite, or secondary effect, that is, increased sensibility, restlessness and sleeplessness, and this is increased with every dose.

What is true of these two remedies, is true of all others. Yet, this is the strange principle on which all Allopathic prescriptions are made, that is, to get the primary effects of medicines, which, if good, are at the best but very brief, and are soon followed by the opposite effect, which, of course, must be bad. Everybody is familiar with the fact, that multitudes of persons, after an Allopathic treatment, are left with lasting and ruinous medicinal diseases, though the medicines may have done them temporary good.

If the public were thoroughly acquainted with thir one law, they would never tolerate another dose of Allopathic medicine for themselves or their families. If the physician should prescribe a laxative or cathartic to remove constipation, the better informed patient would say to him something like this: "My dear sir, as I understand the laws of cure, your dose will give me very transient relief by its primary effect; but the secondary effect will be just the reverse, and will be lasting, so that I shall get only temporary relief, at the expense of a lasting aggravation of the very difficulty from which you propose to relieve me. I really cannot afford to pay such a price for so small a benefit." The same reasoning applies equally to every Allopathic prescription for every disease.

SECOND LAW.—But there is another law equally practical and equally important, viz.: That all medicines produce two exactly opposite effects, according to quantity, that is, small and large doses produce precisely opposite effects. So far is it from being true, that if a small dose will do a little good, a large one will do more, the truth is, that if sa mall dose does good, a large one will certainly do mischief, for the effects of the two are just the opposite of each other For example: a small dose of opium produces wakeful ness and exhileration, while a large dose produces stupor and sleep. Small doses of rhubarb, mercury and other cathartics, allay irritability of the bowels, and cure diarrhœa and dysentery, while large doses, everybody knows, produce precisely opposite effects. Very small doses of ipecac and emetic tartar, allay irritation of the stomach, and stop vomiting and cholera morbus, while large doses produce only irritation and vomiting. The one is the disease-curing, the other disease-producing, effect.

Guided by this law, the physician will so administer his medicines as to secure the disease-curing effect, and avoid the disease-producing effect. Patients, well informed, will be wise enough to refuse a prescription made in violation of this law. But the Allopathic physician always aims to get the primary or disease-producing effect. He knows nothiug of treating disease by any other method. A wise patient will say to a physician, who prescribes for him a large dose of medicine, (and *all* Allopathic doses are large, though they call them small) : "Sir, I consulted you for the purpose of being cured, and you offer me a drug in a dose that will make me sick. The law of cure, as I understand it, makes it no part of the business of a physician to produce disease, but his exclusive business to cure it. The time is past, when the appropriate inscription on a physician's sign was a 'disease manufactory,' and the proper title of the profession—'The *destructive* art of healing.' I must insist on your treating me in harmony with the now well known laws of cure, or I must take the treatment into my own hands, or consult some one better informed."

We can now better understand the reason of the law—"LIKE CURES LIKE." We see a patient laboring under symptoms exactly like those produced by large doses of belladonna. This, then, must be the appropriate remedy, because, in small doses it produces symptoms exactly the opposite of those produced by large doses, and the opposite of those under which the patient labors, and, of course, establishes an opposite effect, that is, in other words, cures the disease.

Is not this law of cure, then, founded on nature, and does it not commend itself to our reason and common sense? And when we see our remedies in small doses prescribed according to this law, perform such wonderful cures, is it notj ust what we ought to expect? We always know *why* we give any certain remedy, and know what its effects will be, for we have tried them in large doses on the healthy, and understand their properties. How different it is with the Allopathic physician? Let us see how he learns to treat a disease. He takes up, for example, the study of fever, with a view of preparing himself to treat it. He reads in his books that one physician recommends cold affusions, and another disagrees with him and thinks them dangerous. One advises wine, and another insist that the patient should have only the most cooling drinks. Many prescribe Peruvian bark or quinine, and others object to these remedies as hurtful. Some recommend a free use of cathartics, and others warn the young physician against their use. Some recommend opiates, others think them dangerous. And so on to the end of the chapter, almost every remedy in the *Materia Medica* being recommended by some and repudiated by others. Thus furnished, the physician goes forth to take the lives of the public in his hands, at full liberty, under high medical authorities, to employ just what remedies he pleases, and sadly puzzled to make a choice. During all his practice, he never has a glimpse of any law to guide him in his perilious work. The best reason he can give for prescribing any of his drugs is, that somebody thinks he has found it useful, without knowing why, in cases that seem similar. It is an unmitigated system of guess-work, and life-and-death-experiment, upon the sick and the suffering. How different is it with the Homœopath! When we see a patient with the symptoms of an ordinary attack of fever, we give Gelseminum, because we have taken it ourselves beforehand, while in health, and know that it produces just that train of symptoms, and therefore *know* that it will *cure* them, and we are not disappointed. In another form of fever, we give Tartar for the same reason and with the same result. We always know *why* we give a remedy, because we have a clear and unmistakeable law to guide us.

We have constantly new diseases, or old diseases putting on new forms. We are prepared for them beforehand. Every Homœopathist knew, years before cholera appeared in this country, that camphor, arsenicum and veratrum would cure it, because these remedies had been proved on the healthy, and found to produce symptoms *like* those of cholera. And when cholera appeared, we treated it with the most triumphant success, from the very first, while Allopathic physicians were experimenting, and their patients dying; and they are still experimenting on this and all other diseases. Even now, after so many years of experimenting, they cannot save half the proportion of patients that Homœopathists saved the very first year of its appearance. Is it strange that a man, with any feeling of humanity, should be anxious to diffuse a knowledge of a system of medicine, possessing so many advantages, and so full of blessings to the sick?

Finally, we feel certain that if the public mind can become imbued with the doctrines of Homœopathy, and generally adopt it in practice, it will be the most effectual remedy for the now all-prevalent and destructive quackery, and be a vast saving of health and life. Try it and then decide on its merits.

LIST OF REMEDIES IN FULL FAMILY CASE.

	NAMES.	STRENGTH.	CONTRACTIONS.
1	Aconitum nap,	Tinct.	Acon... 0
2	Agaricus mus.,	3 pellets.	Agar. 3
3	Ambra grisia,	6 do	Amb. 6
4	Ammonium carb.,	3 trit.	Am. C...... 3
5	Apis mellifica,	3 pel.	Apis. 3
6	Arum triphyl,	3 trit.	Arum. 3
7	Arnica mont.,	Tinct.	Arn........ 0
8	Arsenicum alb.,	6 pel.	Ars......... 6
9	Atropine,	6 do	Atrop...... 6
10	Belladonna,	3 do	Bell........ 3
11	Balsam copaiva,	3 do	Bals. cop... 3
12	Bryonia alba,	3 do	Bry. 3
13	Calendula,	Tinct.	Calend..... 0
14	Calcarea carb.,	6 pel.	Calc........ 6
15	Cantharides,	3 pel.	Canth 3
16	Caulophyllin,	3 trit.	Caul. 3
17	Chamomilla,	3 pel.	Cham...... 3
18	Chelidonium,	3 do	Chel........ 3
19	China	3 do	China. 3
20	Cocculus,	3 do	Coc. 3
21	Colocynth,	3 do	Coloc... ... 3
22	Corallium,	6 pel.	Cor 6
23	Croton tiglium,	6 do	Crot........ 6
24	Dulcamara,	3 do	Dulc. 3
25	Ferrum met.,	6 do	Fer. 6
26	Gelseminum,	Tinct.	Gels........ 0
27	Glanderine,	6 pel.	Gland. 6
28	Graphites,	6 do	Graph...... 6
29	Hamamelis virginica,	Tinct.	Ham. 0
30	Hepar sulphuris,	6 pel.	Hep........ 6
31	Hydrastis Canadensis	Tinct.	Hydras 0
32	Ignatia,	3 pel.	Ig.......... 3
33	Ipecacuanha,	3 do	Ip.......... 3
34	Kali hydriodicum,	6 do	Kal hyd... 6
35	Leptandrin,	3 trit.	Lept. 3
36	Lobelia inflata,	3 pel.	Lob. 3
37	Macrontin,	3 trit.	Mac. 3
38	Mercurins corros,	6 pel.	Merc cor. .. 6
39	Mercurius solub.,	6 do	Merc. sol... 6
40	Nux Vomica,	3 do	Nux. 3
41	Phosphorus,	3 do	Phos. 3
42	Phosphoric acid,	3 do	Phos. ac.. . 3
43	Podophyllin,	3 trit.	Pod.. 3
44	Pulsatilla,	3 pel.	Puls........ 3
45	Rhus tox,	3 do	Rhus.. 3
46	Sepia,	6 do	Sep......... 6
47	Santonine,	3 trit.	Sant. 3
48	Sulphur,	6 pel.	Sulph...... 6
49	Sulphuric acid,	3 do	Sulph. ac .. 3
50	Spongia,	3 do	Spong. 3
51	Tartar stib.,	3 trit.	Tart........ 3
52	Veratrum alb.,	3 pel.	Verat. 3

Case of 32 of the most Important Remedies.

1 Aconitum nap.
2 Ambra grisea.
3 Ammon Carb.
4 Arnica.
5 Arsenicum.
6 Atropine.
7 Belladonna.
8 Bryonia
9 Calendula.
10 Caulophyllin.
11 Chamomilla.
12 Colocynth.
13 Dulcamara.
14 Gelseminum.
15 Hamamelis.
16 Hydrastis.
17 Ipecac.
18 Kali Hyd.
19 Leptandrin.
20 Macrotin.
21 Merc. cor.
22 Merc. sol.
23 Nux Vom.
24 Phosphorus.
25 Podophyllin.
26 Pulsatilla.
27 Rhus. tox.
28 Sulphur.
29 Sulphuric acid.
30 Spongia.
31 Tartar.
32 Veratrum.

Cases of Remedies not found in most Domestic Works or Cases.

1 Ambra.
2 Agaricus.
3 Ammonium carb.
4 Arum.
5 Atropine
6 Bals. cop.
7 Calendula.
8 Caulophyllin
9 Gelseminum
10 Glanderine.
11 Hamamelis.
12 Hydrastis.
13 Leptandrin.
14 Macrotin.
15 Podophyllin.
16 Santonine.

TRAVELING CASE.

1 Arnica.
2 Arsenicum.
3 Belladonna.
4 Colocynth.
5 Gelsemium.
6 Merc. cor.
7 Nux. Vom.
8 Phosphorus.
9 Podophyllin.
10 Veratrum.

PRICES.

52	Remedies,	Case and	Book, Upright,	$7.00
50	do	do	Flat,	6.00
32	do	do	do	4.50
16	do	do	do	2.50
10	do	do	do	1.50

The case of 16 remedies contains those that are not found in most domestic books.

N. B. While taking Homœopathic remedies, the patient should abstain from all other remedies or articles having medicinal properties, either in the form of drugs, herb drinks or diet, as acids, especially vinegar, soda, saleratus, pepper, spice, cinnamon, cloves, &c.; and when the habit is not incorrigible, from green tea, coffee and tobacco.

GENERAL DIRECTIONS.

The usual dose of pellets for an adult is six; for children, from one to four, according to age. When the pellets are dissolved, which is preferable, when convenient, if pure water can be had; put 10 or 12 in a gill of water, and give teaspoonfull doses. When tincture of *Acon.* is used internally, 2 or 3 drops may be put in a gill of water; dose, a teaspoonfull. When grains of the triturations or powders are mentioned, what will lie upon a 3 cent piece may be considered about 2 grains.

The usual dose of a powder, when not otherwise directed, is a grain, or if dissolved, 2 or 3 grains in a gill of water; dose, a teaspoonfull.

When taking Homœopathic remedies, the patient must abstain from all other medicines—herb drinks, odors, as Camphor, Cologne, Hartshorn, &c., and avoid vinegar, pepper and spices, and, as far as possible, coffee and tobacco.

PRACTICAL HOMŒOPATHY

FOR THE PEOPLE.

FEVERS

In a work like this, it would be worse than useless to treat of fevers under the various and numerous names by which they are called in medical books. We shall regard all fevers as one disease, with a number of varieties, and give the treatment for the principal different forms it assumes.

The great majority of fevers in this country are, what are called bilious, or bilious remittent; because they give evidence of bilious disorder, or disordered action of the liver, and have a *remission* every twenty-four hours, that is, a period during which the fever is less. This usually occurs in the morning.

This form of fever, after some days or only hours of languor, loss of appetite, and perhaps nausea, headache and feeling of fatigue, makes its attack by a chill more or less severe, pain in the head, back and limbs, restlessness, a feeling of weakness, bad taste of the mouth and coated tongue. Its course will depend on the treatment. Under the physicking and drugging treatment its course is generally prolonged for several weeks; often assumes at a late stage, a low, typhoid form, and is not unfrequently fatal.

After the chilly stage is over, which may be from one or two to six or eight hours, it is followed by dry heat, continued headache, restlessness, loss of appetite, more or less thirst, and a general feeling of severe sickness. The tongue becomes more coated with a dirty white or yellowish color, the pulse is frequent, often from 100 to 120 in the minute. Towards morning, some remission comes on, and perhaps there is a slight moisture of the skin, the pains are less, and the patient sleeps more quietly. This is repeated from day to day. Sometimes the tongue is dry and of a browner color in the middle. The edges and tip are sometimes red, and sometimes the whole surface of the tongue.

This form of fever, if well drugged, according to the usual Allopathic practice, as I said, is usually prolonged to several weeks. If *no medicine* is given—if the patient entirely abstains from food, and gratifies his thirst with water only, and if the surface is washed frequently, whenever the skin is hot and dry, and the room kept well aired, the fever will generally be ended in from seven to nine days. But under a good Homœopathic treatment, it is usually cured in twenty-four hours, and where this fails, in less than a week.

TREATMENT.—In the early or chilly stage, put a few drops of *Gels.* in a tumbler, and add an equal number of spoonsfull of water, and give a spoonfull every half hour till the chill ceases, and perspiration is procured or the pain and fever subside. Then stop it as long as the improvement continues. As soon as the symptoms begin to return, renew it. In a majority of cases, the first dose stops the chills within fifteen or twenty minutes. If the first dose produces no effect, increase it to 2, 3, or 5 drops, for there is a great difference in the quantity required by different persons. In many cases ½ or ¼ drop is sufficient. After a free perspiration is thus produced, the pains subside and the patient goes to sleep, and when he wakes, is conscious that his fever "is broken up." It is important that this treatment should be adopted in the early stage of the attack. I have cured innumerable cases by this remedy alone. This is applicable to all fevers that come on with chills and pains, as above described, whether catarrhal, or from a cold, bilious, typhoid or rheumatic. When these symptoms are present, *Gels.* is the remedy. If the treatment is not commenced till a later period, it will often succeed, and should be tried as the first remedy, but there is much less certainty of success. But it need not be continued over one day, if it is not obviously doing good. If this fails and the fever puts on the forms and symptoms hereafter described, then corresponding remedies must be used.

Another form of fever comes on slowly and almost imperceptibly, without pain and with only a feeling of languor, of fatigue and aversion to any effort. The mind is dull, and the tongue is either merely coated or it is more or less red at the tip and edges, or it is dry and brownish through the middle. In such cases, if not soon relieved by *Gels.* give *Tartar stib.* (2 grains in a gill of water,) in teaspoonfull doses every 3 hours, and continue it for some days. Under this, there will generally be, after the first 24 hours, a daily abatement, and the fever will subside in a few days. If there is sleeplessness, delirium or headache, give, besides, a dose of *Bell.* three times a day.

In fevers, in which the bilious symptoms are most prominent, such as yellowish coat of the tongue, bitter taste, feeling of fullness or tenderness in the region of the liver, along the edges of the lower ribs of the right side and pit of the stomach, costiveness, or bilious diarrhœa, high colored urine, and feeling of nausea at the stomach, *Pod.* or *Bry.* and *Nux.* are the remedies. One may be given alone, or both alternately, three hours apart. If, however, the fever is high, and there is a good deal of pain in any internal organ, *Aconite* must be given, either alone or alternated with *Bry.*, until these symptoms are subdued. And here is a good place to remark, that while *Gels.* is the best remedy known for simple fever, *Acon.* is the indispensable remedy for local inflammations, which often exist in in fever. This distinction is of great importance, and should not be forgotten.

If the fever has assumed a low, typhoid character, with delirium, great weakness, dry lips, which, with the teeth, are covered with a dark crust, twitching of the tendons, and picking at the bed-clothes, give *Ars.* and *Bell.* or *Ars.* and *Hydr.*, 3 hours apart.

Under this treatment, very few fevers will continue a

week. In the severe fevers it is of great importance to have fresh air passing frequently over a patient's bed to carry off the effluvia constantly arising from the body. It has long been observed in hospitals, that patients with fevers did not do as well who were placed in a corner where a *current* of air could not pass over them. The whole surface should be sponged over several times a day with water of a temperature to be agreeable to the feeling. Once a day there may be a little saleratus, or soda, or ley from ashes added to the water. During the continuance of the fever there should be a total abstinence from food, except water gruel, rice-water, barley water, or similar things, made very thin for a drink; and even these had better be omitted for several days, and only water given. The linen and bed-clothes should be changed daily. The patient should be kept entirely quiet, undisturbed by noise, and especially by conversation, and the room should be cool and not disagreeably light. After recovery commences, if the bowels are costive, give a dose of *Nux. v.* every night.

Intermittent Fever---Chill Fever.

TREATMENT.—During the chill and fever, give *Gels.* as above. During the intermission, if there is bilious derangement such as coated tongue, impaired appetite, head-ache and feeling of illness, give *Ipecac.* and *Pod.* alternately every three or four hours; or *Ipecac* and *Nux.* for a man, and *Ipecac* and *Puls.* for woman and children.

Within a few days, by this treatment, the disordered state during the intermission, will generally subside, and the patient will feel tolerably well, except during the chill and fever. Then, if the chills and fever continue, give, during the intermission, *Ars.* every 3 or 4 hours. But few cases will continue many days under this treatment, unless complicated with other disorders. Many cases that have been treated for months with Quinine, will be cured by this simple course in a few days.

From thirty years observation and experience of Quinine, I am perfectly convinced that it has done infinitely more mischief than the ague would have done, if left entirely to itself. It undoubtedly stops the chills, and the fever temporarily; but these are only two symptoms of a general disease, which remains after the chills have stopped, with a more serious Quinine disease added to it. Thousands have thus *cured* an ague a dozen times in the course of a season, which, after all, still remained, in an aggravated and more dangerous form than at first. If *Ars.* fails to cure it in a few days, give *China* in the same manner.

Scarlatina—Scarlet Fever.

This comes on with many of the symptoms of other fevers. After a short time, the pulse becomes very quick—often, in children, 120 to 140 in the minute. The skin is hotter than in any other disease. The scarlet eruption comes out over the body on the second day, but may be seen in thickly scattered, red points over the tongue on the first day. The excess of fever often produces delirium. There is usually some soreness of the throat. This is the simplest form of the disease and the mildest.

TREATMENT.—*Aconite* and *Bell.* are the chief remedies, alternated every 2 or 3 hours. Whenever the skin is very hot and dry, it should be frequently bathed all over with water of a temperature to suit the feelings of the patient. This, if frequently done, in a remarkable degree, diminishes the fever and quiets the nervous irritability. After a good bathing, the patient will frequently recover from his delirium, become quiet and fall asleep, while the pulse falls from 10 to 20 in the minute. I have practiced this free bathing in this disease, frequently with cold water, for thirty years. The fear that will make the eruption "strike in," is totally without foundation. A chill should, of course, be avoided.

Scarlatina Anginosa.

This is a more severe form of the disease in which soreness and swelling of throat is a prominent symptom. The throat is swollen inside and out. Swallowing is painful and difficult. If the inner surface of the throat is examined, it will be found red, inflamed and often covered with a membrane, in patches of a dirty white, or ash, or yellowish color. The fever is high and the pulse quick. There is more prostration of strength than in the simple form, and more pains.

TREATMENT.—*Aconite* and *Bell.* are still the remedies in the early stage, alternated every hour or two. If ulcers appear in the throat, or if it is much swollen, omit the *Acon.* and give *Bell.* and *Merc. Cor.* for men, or *Merc. Sol.* for women and children. If the throat remains ulcerated for some days, after the fever has somewhat subsided, omit these remedies and give *Hydr.* (10 drops in a gill of water,) in teaspoonfull doses, every 2 or 3 hours, and gargle the throat after each dose, with a wash of the same, a teaspoonfull to a gill. I have very recently seen the most beautiful effects from this use of *Hydr.* in cases where the throat was badly ulcerated.

Malignant Scarlatina.

This is a still more dangerous form of the disease. The prostration of strength is much greater, the pulse weak and quick—the throat dark red and ulcerated—there is extremely bad, fetid breath—the nostrils are often excoriated or raw with a fetid, acrid discharge, and there is a tendency to gangrene of the throat and general sinking.

TREATMENT.—When these symptoms appear, give several doses of *Amon. carb*, 2 grains in a gill of water, a teaspoonfull every hour or two. This will frequently change the dark threatening color of the throat and other corresponding symptoms, in a short time. Follow this with *Hydr.* as above, for a gargle, and give *Ars.* every 2 or 3 hours. Most of the cases, even of malignant scarlet fever, will be cured by this treatment. I need not say how hopeless they are with the commor treatment.

In the worst forms of the disease with obstinate tendency to gangrene, if other remedies fail, *Glanderine* should be given every hour or two. It is a powerful remedy. It is said, on good authority, "In terrible cases of Scarlatina, where the odor of the breath is putrid, and the mouth and throat are filled with tenacious mucus, while the swollen tonsils close the throat, this remedy alone, seems capable of rescuing the patient." In all malignant and gangrenous ulcerations, it is a remedy of great power.

The treatment given for this disease, in its malignant form, is equally applicable to the disease which has appeared in several parts of the country under the name of the "black tongue," or malignant erysipelas. For dropsy, that some times follows Scarlatina, *Ars.* every 4 hours.

DIPTHERIA.

This disease has some resemblance, in character and symptoms, to Malignant Scarlatina. From its late prevalenceand its frequent fatality, it is very important that its symptoms and treatment should be well understood. In its simplest forms, it usually comes on with chilliness, fever and languor. These symptoms are attended with redness, heat and soreness of the throat, and more or less pain on swallowing. When it appears only in this simple form, *Bell.* every 2 hours, is the appropriate remedy; or, if there is much feverish heat, alternate with *Acon.* If the throat is red and sore, a gargle of a teaspoonfull of tincture of *Bell.* to a tumbler of water, after each dose of *Bell.* has a charming effect. But if the disease goes on, there are soon other symptoms. There is more or less swelling of the throat, externally and internally, the nose is stoped and discharges a thin or ropy mucus, the patient is more prostrate and languid, and complains of general soreness or lameness. When these symptoms occur, give *Bell.* and *Merc.* every hour or two.

But there is often sickness of the stomach, with pain and tenderness on pressure, great weakness, sweating or moist skin, with patches of false membrane over various parts of the throat of an ash or straw color. Sometimes these patches are very small—mere points and few—sometimes numerous and large. With these symptoms there is fetid breath and often fetid discharge from the nose. In this condition *Am. carb.* is indispensable, 3 or 4 grains in a gill of water, teaspoonfull doses every hour, for 5 or 6 hours. Then if the membrane is not thrown off, *Merc.* and *Bell.* alternated every hour or two. When the glands are much swollen and the breath very fetid, *Glanderine*, as in Malignant Scarlatina, may save the patient when other remedies fail. In these worst cases, gargle the throat with the *Hyd.* and if there is great prostration or diarrhœa give it as in Scarlatina.

There are other remedies often important as *Nitric* and *Sulfuric Acid, Bromine* and *Iodine*, which are difficult to be kept by families for use. Indeed this formidable disease should be in the hands of a physician whenever a competent one can be had. If the patient complains of heat and burning in the throat, there is no gargle so good as *Cayenne Pepper* in water, of considerable strength, every 2 or 3 hours, at the same time giving teaspoonfull doses between, till the burning sensation ceases.

MEASLES.

This comes on with languor, a coarse, harsh cough, watery eyes, and fever, with pains in the limbs, headache and chilliness. The eruption appears about the fourth day, but before this it may be seen on the roof of the mouth and throat. The remedy from the first is *Gels.*, but in smallar doses than in fever, 3 drops in a tumbler of water, a teaspoonfull every 2 or 3 hours, till the fever subsides. If the cough should remain troublesome, *Bry.*, *Puls.*, or *Phos.*, every 3 or 4 hours.

The fever accompanying the measles cannot be at once "broken up," like other fevers, but can be greatly moderated during its course by *Gels.*, and the eruption under its use is often but trifling. If there is troublesome dry cough or nausea, or diarrhœa, *Ipecac.*

ERYSEPILAS

Consists in a diffused, rather dark redness of the skin, with itching, burning and fever. It appears in three forms, the simple, vescicular, and phlegmonous.

It often appears about the head and face, and is then a dangerous disease.

TREATMENT.—In the simple form, consisting of a simple diffused redness without great swelling, *Bell.* alone, or alternated with *Acon.*, is sufficient every 2, 3 or 4 hours.

In the vescicular form, that is, where blisters rise on the inflamed skin, if it is on the head and face, *Bell.* and *Rhus.* If on other parts, the same, or *Rhus.* and *Graph.*

In the phlegmonous form, that is, when the pain is deep seated, and the inflammation extends beyond the skin, into the parts beneath, with a good deal of swelling and severe pain, the two last remedies are good, but *Apis Mel.* is probably the most reliable remedy. It may be given alone, or alternated with *Bell.* or *Rhus.* every 2 or 3 hours.

In all the forms of Erysepilas, an application of fresh mashed cranberries, will have an excellent effect.

RHEUMATISM.

We need not occupy space in describing this, as every one recognizes it.

TREATMENT.—If it is attended with severe pain, redness and swelling and fever, especially if it comes on rather suddenly with chills, give *Gels.* By keeping up a perspiration with this for a short time, the disease will frequently be terminated. If not, give *Acon.* and *Bell.* alternately every 2 or 3 hours. When the inflammation has become somewhat diminished, give *Mac.*, a grain every 2 or 3 hours, and continue it as long as it is obviously doing good, or *Bry.* in the same manner.

Sometimes Rheumatism changes its place from one part to another. In this case, give *Bry.* and *Puls*, 2 or 3 hours apart.

If there is profuse sweating which does not relieve, but only weakens the patient, as sometimes occurs in this disease, give *Merc. cor.* for men, or *Merc. sol.* for women and children, every 2 or 3 hours till this state is corrected.

This treatment will cure a majority of cases quicker than they usually are cured, but there are chronic and complicated cases of Rheumatism, which require skill and experience. If the disease has been of long standing, electricity becomes an indispensable aid.

NEURALGIA—PAIN OF A NERVE.

The locality of this disease is very various, and wherever located, very distressing. One side of the face or head, is a very common location. It occurs most frequently in feeble and nervous females.

Treatment.—A majority of the cases will be promptly relieved by *Gels.*, but it sometimes requires to be given in pretty large doses, repeated every half hour till the pain is relieved. *Acon.* in drop doses of the tincture, and a wash of equal parts of the same and water, applied over the painful nerve, is often equally effectual; but if any feeling of numbness is produced, it should be at once stopped.

This disease usually consists of paroxysms with intervals of ease. During these intervals give *Ars.* every 2 or 3 hours.

If connected with disordered menstruation or female difficulties, *Mac. Puls.* and *Sep.* during the intervals, only one at a time, every 3 or 4 hours.

INFLAMMATIONS.

Inflammation of the Tongue.

This is not a very common disease, but requires very prompt attention. The end of the tongue first becomes red and swollen, and in a few hours the whole tongue becomes so large that it protrudes from the mouth.

TREATMENT.—*Merc.* every 2 or 3 hours till improvement is obvious, then less and less frequently. If there is much fever, give *Acon.* between the doses of *Merc.*

When inflammation of the mouth and tongue, with ulceration of the gums, is produced by Mercury, as is often the case in the old practice, give *Hydr.*, and wash the mouth with the same before each dose, with an occasional dose of *Hepar.*

Inflammation of the Throat, or Sore Throat from a Cold.

In the first stage, a few doses of *Gels.* will often effect a very speedy cure. If not, *Arum* every 2 or 3 hours. If the throat becomes ulcerated, a gargle of *Hydr.* frequently, as in scarlet fever.

Inflammation of the Tonsils—Quinzy.

In this disease, the tonsils or glands in the throat, on one or both sides, are inflamed, red, sore and painful.

The pain often extends to the ears. It is produced by a cold.

TREATMENT.—*Acon.* and *Bell.* while there is much fever. If there is but little fever, *Bell.* and *Merc.* If not soon improved, *Arum.* or *Apis.*, or both alternately. In those subject to the attacks of Quinzy, it will usually be avoided by washing the neck every morning with cold water, and rubbing it well, and gargling the throat with the same.

Inflammation of the Stomach—Gastritis.

This is distinguished by pain of the stomach, usually with a burning sensation internally, and tenderness to pressure, vomiting, especially when any food or drink is taken, a feeling of great prostration, thirst, and often cold extremities. The tip and edges of the tongue are red, and sometimes the whole tongue.

TREATMENT.—First give one or two doses of *Acon.* Then *Ars.*, not more than 3 pellets in a gill of water, a teaspoonfull every 3 hours.

If it is connected with indigestion of improper food, *Nux.* alternated with *Ars.*

If the patient becomes greatly reduced, with cold extremities, *Ars.* and *Verat.*

Inflammation of the Bowels—Enteritis.

By this, we mean inflammation of the outer or peritoneal coat of the bowels. It usually comes on like other inflammatory diseases, with a chill. This is accompanied or followed by pain over some part or the whole of the abdomen, which is sharp and severe, often burning. The abdomen becomes sensitive and painful to the least pressure, and is more or less enlarged or swollen. A full breath is painful. There is often vomiting; the face is pale, and looks anxious and suffering. The breathing is short and quick, and the pulse quick and small: it is dangerous, and may be fatal in 2 or 3 days.

Treatment.—During the early stage, give *Gels.* as in fever, and keep up a perspiration for some time, till the pain and fever abate. But if this fails of giving some relief after a few hours, give *Acon.* and *Bell.* alternately every 2 hours, till the violence of the disease abates; afterwards *Bell.* and *Merc.* every 3 or 4 hours. After the patient is fairly recovering, if there is constipation, give *Nux* at bed-time.

Throughout the disease, cloths wrung out of moderately cool water, laid on the bowels and covered with flannel, and copious *hot* water injections greatly aid the cure.

DIARRHŒA.

Under this head, we do not include the disease in infants. In ordinary cases, if it is produced by improper food, *Nux.* and *Ipecac* for men, and *Puls.* and *Ipecac* for women. A dose after each evacuation will be all that is necessary.

If the discharges are copious and watery, *Ars.* If not soon improved, *Ars.* and *Verat.*, or *Phos. acid.*

If the evacuations are billious, yellow, green or dark, *Merc.* or *Pod.*, or both alternately.

If they contain undigested food, *Ars.* or *China*, or *Phos.* acid, a dose, in all cases, after each evacuation.

If the disease is at all bad, the patient should remain quiet in bed and abstain from food till cured.

If the disease has been of long standing, *Sulph.* may sometimes be necessary. But generally it will be cured by *Ars.* or *Pod.* and *Lep.* alternately.

A patient who applied to me for a diarrhœa of two years standing, contracted in Panama, and who had paid over $500 to allopathic physicians without benefit, was cured with a small vial of *Ars.* When the disease has continued a long time and the bowels much weakened, *Hydr.* is a very effectual remedy.

DYSENTERY.

This consists in inflammation of the mucous membrane of the lower portion of the bowels, and is distinguished by slimy and bloody evacuations with pain and tenesmus or straining, without discharging any of the natural contents of the bowels.

TREATMENT.—The principal remedy is *Merc.* after each evacuation. If pain extends over the bowels, or griping, give *Coloc.* alternately with *Merc.*

When this griping is alleviated, if there is no natural evacuation—only bloody mucus, or if there are passages of little hard balls, give *Merc.* and *Nux.* If the disease has become established, do not be in a hurry to change this treatment, for it may require some days to effect a change.

If nausea or vomiting occurs, give *Ipecac* with the *Merc.*, or if there is much thirst with the nausea, *Ars.* till the sickness subsides.

An injection of warm water several time a day, does a good deal of good.

If, after a time, the evacuations are sometimes billious, yellow, brown or dark, give *Pod.* or *China.*

In dysentery of long standing, *Pod.* and *Lep.*, alternately, are effectual remedies.

SEA SICKNESS.

TREATMENT.—A dose of *Nux.*, taken half an hour before going on board will frequently prevent this for some time. When it is felt, *Nux.*, *Ipecac.*, *Ars.*, *Puls.* and *Mac.* are very effectual remedies. One agrees better with some persons, and another with others. Armed with these remedies none need suffer much from sea-sickness. In obstinate cases, *Petroleum* and *Silicia* are sometimes necessary.

I have repeatedly provided foreign missionaries and others, about to cross the ocean, with these remedies, and have received very warm acknowledgments for the comforts they conferred and the great good they were able to do their fellow passengers with them.

COLIC—STOMACH ACHE.

TREATMENT.—If this arises from indigestion or improper food, *Nux.* or *Puls.* If from cold drinks, ice cream, &c., *Ars.*

In *billious* colic with violent pain coming on in paroxysms with disposition to bend forward, *Coloc.* in pretty large doses is a most prompt remedy, often curing the most violent colic almost instantaneously. If necessary it may be repeated in a few minutes.

If there is great restlessness and billious vomiting or diarrhœa, *Cham.* or *Pod.* In flatulent colic, or colic from wind, *Coloc.*, *Cocculus* or *Cham.*

WORMS AND WORM DISEASES.

TREATMENT.—*Santonine,* 1 grain, not to be repeated under two days. If this produces no effect, give 2 grains, then 3 grains or more. This is usually the only remedy needed and does no mischief, and is more effectual than all the pink and senna, calomel, &c., of the shops. But what are believed to be worm symptoms are often the result of indigestion and improper food, and are cured by *Nux.*, *Ipecac* and *Pod.*

Tape-Worm.

TREATMENT.—Drink freely of an infusion of pumpkin seeds bruised—Pumpkin seed tea. There is abundant testimony of the efficacy of this simple remedy in expelling tape-worm.

PILES—HEMORRHOIDS.

This disease consists in enlarged veins filled with blood, either within the bowel or just outside of the opening, or both. The tumours thus formed, often become very painful, inflamed, and tender.

TREATMENT.—If the tumours are external and very painful and sore, apply cloths wet in hot water. If not soon relieved, apply a tobacco poultice warm. This, in the worst cases, will produce temporary relief. If it produces any sickness, remove it at once. In the mean time give *Acon.* and *Bell.* half an hour apart. Continue this external and internal treatment till the violent pain and soreness are abated.

The tumours should not be permitted to remain protruded externally as it gives rise to great suffering and mischief. They should be oiled, and by careful pressure, returned entirely within the bowel, and secured there by a compress and bandage.

As constipation always increases the difficulty, the bowels must be kept in a healthy state. This is to be done by a regulated diet, brown bread, fruits, &c., and avoiding all stimulating drinks and high seasoned food, and by appropriate medicines. *Nux.* at night, and *Pod.* in the morning, will generally remove both the constipation and the tendency to piles. If not, *Nux.* one night, and *Sulph.* the next, continued for some time. I have cured cases of 20 years standing by this course.

In bleeding piles, if the bleeding is at all profuse, take *Phos.*, and if not relieved in a few hours, *Hamamelis*, 1 drop every hour, and if nececsary, injections of a gill of water and 10 drops of the same.

Avoid physic in this disease. If necessary, it is infinitely better to use an occasional injection of water.

Lep. is another excellent remedy in this disease, twice a day.

CHOLERA MORBUS.

This is characterized by an attack of vomiting and diarrhœa of billious matter, with pain and cramp of the stomach and bowels. It is very distressing and may be dangerous, but is very quickly cured by Homœopathic treatment.

TREATMENT.—*Ipecac* alone, repeated every 10 or 15 minutes, is generally very quickly effectual. If the pain of the stomach and bowels is considerable, *Coloc.* may be alternated with *Ipecac.* This relieves the pain while *Ipecac* stops the vomiting. If the patient has become much weakened, and the above does not promptly relieve, give *Ars.*, and if the diarrhœa is at all obstinate, *Ars.* and *Verat.* alternately.

ASIATIC CHOLERA.

In the commencement of the attack, a few doses of camphor, in doses of a drop, will often arrest it. If it does not, if vomiting is the most prominent symptom, *Ipecac* every 10 or 15 minutes is often effectual.

But if there are copious rice-water evacuations by the bowels, and vomiting of the same, with thirst and prostration, the chief reliance is to be placed upon *Ars.* and *Verat.*, alternately, every 15 or 20 minutes. These are the only remedies generally required.

Thousands have been cured by these few remedies by the peasantry of Europe, while from half to two-thirds of all the cases were fatal under allopathic treatment. It has everywhere been wonderfully successful.

JAUNDICE.

Is marked by yellowness of the skin and eyes, with languor, weakness, loss of appetite, coated tongue and often head-ache. The urine is high colored and makes a yellow stain on the linen, and the evacuations from the bowels are a light clay color.

TREATMENT.—The remedies are *Leptand.*, *Merc.*, *Chin.*, *Pod.*, and *Nux.* Either of these may be taken separately, or any two of them alternately every 3 to 6 hours till an improvement commences, (which will seldom exceed a few days,) then less frequently. By these remedies the disease is cured vastly quicker, and the system is left in a vastly better condition than under the old mercurial treatment.

This is a disordered state of the liver which may be inflamed, for which see

INFLAMMATION OF THE LIVER—HEPATITES.

This is known by pain just under the edges of the lower ribs of the right side and pit of the stomach, with tenderness on pressure. There is often a feeling of fulness in this region, pain on taking a deep breath, and a sympathetic pain in the right shoulder. If it proceeds very far, there is obvious enlargement of the liver producing a visible fullness in the region, constant dull or sharp pain, and a good deal of fever. There is a loss of appetite, perhaps nausea and billious vomiting; the bowels are costive, or there is looseness, with discharges of unnatural color from unhealthy bile. The skin and eyes are often somewhat tinged with yellow. There is often a dry hacking cough. It frequently comes on with a chill.

TREATMENT.—In the early stage, *Gels.* is the most likely to "break up" the disease by copious perspiration. This remedy has the advantage of acting very quickly, so that if it fails, as it seldom does, not much time is lost. Two or three doses will determine whether the expected effect is to be realized, the dose repeated every half hour. If it produces perspiration, or abates the fever and pain, it should be continued as long as it does good. If it fails, *Acon.* and *Bell.* may be given every 2 hours till the acuteness of the disease is abated. If some soreness and pain remain, the remedies are, *Bell.*, *Merc.*, *Nux.*, *China* and *Pod.*

Bell. is preferable if there is restlessness, fullnes or pain of the head, fullness at the pit of the stomach, difficult breathing, thirst or dizziness.

Merc. if there is yellowness of the skin, bitter taste and tendency to chilliness:

Pod. for the same symptoms and irregular, loose state of the bowels, or nausea.

Nux. if there is considerable tenderness of the liver, thirst, red urine, and constipation.

China applies to almost all the above symptoms, especially if there is considerable weakness. Either of these remedies may be given every three or four hours.

BILLIOUSNESS.

This is not a scientific term, but one which most persons understand. It is like Jaundice, an affection of the liver and pretty closely related to it. One feels languid, dull, sleepy, especially after dinner; he gets easily tired, his appetite gets impaired; often there is dull head-ache and tendency to constipation, and the complexion loses its freshness and becomes of a dull or dirty appearance. People generally understand that these are billious symptoms. They are not unfrequently the precursors of billious fever or jaundice.

People having these symptoms generally suppose that they need a "cleaning out," and accordingly take billious pills or some other physic, which often results in a "fit of sickness." We can point out what all will find "a more excellent way," when they try it.

TREATMENT.—*Pod.* is generally the only necessary remedy. A single dose will often remove all these unpleasant feelings in a few hours. If not, continue it 3 times a day in doses of a grain. If there is a tendency to chilliness or an inactive state of the bowels, after a day take *Nux.* at night and *Pod.* in the morning. This course, for a short time, will save a fit of sickness and a doctor's bill.

DYSPEPSIA—INDIGESTION.

The symptoms of dyspepsia are very numerous. Feeling of a load in the stomach after meals, sour eructation, heart-burn, pain of the stomach, throwing up the food, dullness and pain of the head, low spirits, nervous symptoms, &c.

TREATMENT.—For present relief from the effects of too hearty a meal, *Nux.* or *Puls.* every hour till relieved. For permanent effect—if there is constipation with the other symptoms—*Nux.* before each meal, or for women, *Puls.*

In ordinary cases either *Nux.*, *Puls.*, *Phos.* or *Pod.* before each meal will be appropriate. For heart-burn *Nux.* and *Pod.* alone, or in alternation, with *Phos.*

A regulated diet, the avoidance of stimulating drinks and tonic medicines, bitters, &c., of highly seasoned food and physic, are indispensible.

One need not expect to be cured of dyspeysia by drugging.

In chronic cases, when the stomach has become very much weakened, the use of electricity will often expedite the cure in the most charming manner, and save months of treatment, or an entire failure.

Those of sedentery habits, must abandon confinement and take free exercise in the open air daily.

Daily bathing with cool water, rubbing the surface well, especially over the stomach and bowels is of great service.

COLDS.

Cold in the Head—Coryza, and Cold affecting the Bronchiæ—Bronchitis, Bronchial Catarrh—Cold on the Lungs.

TREATMENT.—If a cold affecting any of these parts comes on with a chill, or with soreness or rawness of the throat, wind-pipe or bronchiæ extending into the chest, or fever, *Gels.* is the prompt and sovereign remedy. A single dose will often "break up" the violence of the disease, remove the inflammation and soreness, and leave only a mild loose cough, which will only require a few doses of *Bry.* or *Puls.* The patient with a cold at all severe should go to bed and keep quiet and warm till better. Medicine produces a vastly better effect when the patient is in bed, and keeps in a quiet and passive state than when he is moving about.

If a cold is confined to the head, with stoppage of the nose, *Nux.* is the remedy every 2 or 3 hours till relieved.

If there is profuse, watery or acrid discharge from the nose, *Kali hyd.* is perhaps the best remedy, but *Ars.* and *Merc.* are effectual.

If there is a rough, raw, sore feeling of the throat or chest, with tightness, oppressed breathing and painful cough, *Gels.* is *the* remedy till these symptoms subside. *Kali hyd.* and *Phos.* are good remedies. When only a loose, painless cough remains, *Bry.*, *Merc.* or *Puls.* will soon complete the cure. Abstain from food as in fever till the cold is relieved. If there is deep soreness of the chest and fever, *Chel.* and *Phos.* in alternation are the best remedies.

INFLUENZA.

Is only an aggravated form of the above affection, prevailing periodically and epidemically.

TREATMENT.—Similar to the above—*Gels.* is the first remedy. If the symptoms are severe, *Ars.* and *Merc.* In the worst and alarming form *Glanderine* is the most reliable remedy, every 2 hours till there is some abatement, then less frequently.

INFLAMMATION OF THE LUNGS—PNEUMONIA.

This is distinguished from the preceding affection of the bronchiæ by the following symptoms:

It usually comes on with a chill, followed by high fever, a full, strong, quick pulse, short difficult breathing, a *dull* pain in one side of the chest, generally the right, which prevents a full breath, white coated tongue and red cheeks. The pain in the side is sometimes changeable in its location for hours before it settles into one fixed place. There is cough from the first. The expectoration is, at first, white and viscid, or sticky and tough; at a later period it is reddish or brick colored. If there was doubt before, as to the nature of the disease, there need be no longer, after this reddish expectoration appears, for this is a sure sign of inflammation on the lungs.

TREATMENT.—In the first stage of the disease, as in

most other inflammatory diseases, *Gels.* is capable o. breaking up the disease in the first 24 hours by producing free perspiration. Repeat it as occasion requires till the fever and pain abate. If cough remains, with or without a little pain on taking a full breath, give *Phos.* or *Bry.* every 2 or 3 hours.

Aconite and *Phos.* have been hitherto relied upon in the acute stage, and they are effectual remedies—seldom failing to cure Pneumonia in 3 or 4 days, but *Gels.* is much more prompt and effectual if given at an early stage.

If the disease has been neglected during the early stage, and has become established, it is, of course, not so quickly cured, but even then, instead of continuing three weeks and being f..tal in a large proportion of cases, as under the old treatment, it will generally be cured, by following the course here prescribed, in less than a week, and never be fatal unless in very diseased or dilapidated constitutions.

When the disease is thus advanced, before the treatment is commenced, give *Gels.* as above. If it produces relief of the fever and pain by sweating or otherwise, continue it as long as improvement goes on. If it fails to produce a good effect after 5 or 6 doses, stop it and give *Acon.* and *Phos.*, two hours apart, till there is an obvious improvement, then less frequently till the pain and fever have pretty much subsided. If the patient does not improve in 12 hours, give *Chel.* and *Phos.*, in the same manner, or these may be given at first, instead of *Acon.* and *Phos.* All inflammations have a forming or congestive stage, in which there may be chills, and low pulse. This is the stage in which *Gels.* will break up the disease. After this stage is past, and high fever, and fixed, local pain come on, we must resort to *Aconite*, or other proper remedies. If some pain on taking a deep breath remains, then give *Bry.* every 3 or 4 hours for a day or two. If any difficulty remains, then give *Sulph.* three times a day. But in all cases continue the remedy given as long as the patient improves under it.

In every stage, a wet cloth, moderately cool, over the chest, well covered with flannel to avoid any chilliness, aids the cure.

In some cases the cough remains dry an unusual length of time after the attack, with very little expectoration, with great oppression of the chest and difficult breathing. In this case, *Tart. stib.* is the best remedy to bring on expectoration or loosen the cough, every hour or two till relieved.

PLEURISY.

This consists of inflammation of the pleura or covering membrane of the lungs. It has many of the general symptoms of Pneumonia, but the pain in the side is sharp, acute, stitching, instead of dull. It is impossible to take a full breath on account of this sharp pain. The pulse is sharper and smaller—there is less expectoration, and it is not bloody, unless it be some small *streaks* of blood. Not unfrequently the two diseases are combined, constituting what is called pleuro-pneumonia.

THE TREATMENT does not differ from that of Pneumonia.

BLEEDING FROM THE LUNGS.

TREATMENT.—If there is much fever, *Acon.* every hour till moderated, then *Hamam*, 1 drop every hour or half hour, or even one fourth hour, according to urgency. If there is sore bruised feeling of the chest, *Arn.* is an appropriate remedy. If there is much weakness, with irritation of the lungs, *Phos.* acid.

ASTHMA.

Confirmed asthma is a difficult disease to cure. The principal remedies are *Ars.* and *Ipecac.* Either of these may be given, during aparoxysm every hour, till relieved. In nervous or hysterical women, *Acon.*, *Bell.* or *Ambra* sometimes give relief. Distressing paroxysms are sometimes promptly relieved by sufficient doses of *Lobelia* to produce nausea. *Gels.* sometimes affords very prompt relief, especially if brought on by a cold.

But the change of climate or locality affects the greatest number of cures. Many persons afflicted with it at the East, are permanently relieved on removing to the West. Horses affected with Heaves, a similar disease, so as to be rendered useless at the East, are often entirely cured on being taken upon the Western prairies. This is one of the diseases that is often most promptly relieved and eventually cured by electricity. Persons who have not been able to lie down for weeks, are sometimes able to do so from a single application.

COUGH.

This sometimes exists without obvious inflammation. If not of a consumptive character, *Bry.*, *Phos.*, *Puls.*, *Balsam cop.*, *Mac.* or *Arum* may be taken 2 or 3 times a day.

Hoarseness, without fever, will be removed by *Arum*, *Spongia*, *Hepar.*, *Phos.*, or *Kali hyd.*

INFLAMMATION OF THE KIDNEYS—NEPHRITIS.

This usually comes on like most inflammatory diseases, with a chill, accompanied or followed by pain in the back, not in the spine, but on one or both sides of it, that is, in the location of the kidneys, tenderness on pressure in this region, fever, nausea, often vomiting, the urine scanty and high colored, often bloody—the bowels constipated. The pain often extends down to the groin and neck of the bladder.

TREATMENT.—*Gels.*, as in other inflammatory diseases, in the early stage, is the remedy, continued as long as it gives relief. This, if commenced early, will "break it up" by perspiration.

If this has been neglected, or if the disease has continued for some time, and *Gels.* fails of producing the desired effect, and the pain shoots from the kidneys down to the bladder, and there is colicky pain, give *Bell.* every hour or two.

If there are shooting, tearing or cutting pains, with very scanty urine, which is passed with pain, *Canth.* every 2 or 3 hours. In general these two remedies may be given to advantage, alternately.

During the treatment, the bowels should be freely moved by copious injections of water, and make a free use of the warm hip-baths, that is, sitting in a tub of quite warm water, deep enough to come up over the hips.

INFLAMMATION OF THE BLADDER — CYSTITS.

This comes on with the same general symptoms as the last disease, with pain in the bladder, constant desire to pass urine, which is very scanty at each discharge, often bloody, and passed with terrible pain, often with nausea and vomiting. There is a feeling of weight in the region of the bladder, and tenderness to pressure.

Treatment.—The treatment is nearly the same as that of Nephritis. If not soon relieved by *Gels.* in the first stage, give *Acon.* every hour till the fever is somewhat abated, and the most distressing symptoms somewhat moderated, then *Can'h.* every 2 or 3 hours.

The baths and injections, as in Nephritis, are still more useful here.

INFLAMMATION OF THE BRAIN.

This disease is characterized by pain of the head, rolling the head from side to side, dilated or contracted pupils, throbbing of the arteries of the neck and temples, delirium, drowsiness or stupor. There is fever with quick pulse. It is very apt to end in convulsions when fatal.

TREATMENT.—The chief remedies are *Acon.*, ***Bell.*** and *Bry.* Give the two first, alternately, every two hours till the fever and other symptoms are somewhat abated; then *Bell.* and *Bry.* every 3 hours. Persevere in this treatment even though the improvement may not be very perceptible. Do not irritate and torment the patient with blisters, mustard plaisters or any other irritating applications. Shut out all strong light, avoid all noise, and especially conversation within hearing of the patient, (and the hearing is very acute in this disease); keep the room well aired and of comfortably cool temperature, and disturb and excite the patient as little as possible. Do not apply cold water to the head. I have been entirely satisfied for years, that vastly more mischief than good is done by cold applications in this disease. Cloths wet in ***hot*** water may be now and then applied for a short time only, with benefit; keep the bowels free by injections of water, and keep the feet warm. Sponge over the surface of the body with warm water, if the patient is hot and restless.

HEAD-ACHE.

Head-ache arises from a great variety of causes and is attended by such a variety of complications and constitutional conditions, that it is difficult to prescribe, except for individual cases. Each case is a study by itself. We can only give some general directions, which will, however, be found to apply to a great number of individual cases.

1st. It is often produced by indigestion or disordered stomach. This often goes under the name of sick head-ache.

TREATMENT.—*Nux.* will often promptly cure such cases if taken when the symptoms are first felt. *Pod.* and *Ipecac* are often equally good, and for women, *Puls.* The same may be said of *Mac.*, for women. *Nux.* at night, and *Pod.* in the morning will often prevent it in those subject to it.

2d. It often occurs in females as an essentially nervous disease, and is generally called nervous head-ache. In these cases *Mac.*, *Puls.* and *Sepia* are frequently efficient remedies, and when relieved, an occasional dose of one or the other of these will prevent its recurrence

If connected with female weakness, or accompanying monthly disorders, the last three remedies are specially applicable.

If connected with a hysterical state, *Mac.* or *Cocculus.* If produced by grief, *Ignatia.* Either may be taken every hour or two till relief is obtained. A dose of *Mac.*, *Sep.* or *Puls.*, daily, will often do much to prevent these attacks. But a remedy of extraordinary power, and which will cure a larger proportion of what are called nervous and sick head-aches than, perhaps, any other, is *Atropine.* I have cured with it, great numbers of cases that have resisted all other treatment, some of 15 or 20 years standing. It is *most* applicable to those cases that are not caused by disordered stomach or other affection, but depends on a disordered condition of the nervous system itself; to cases that come on rather suddenly, and are very acute and severe. It may be taken every 10 or 15 minutes till an effect is felt. Increase the dose if necessary. As soon as an effect is felt, suspend it till the effect ceases or while improvement continues. If an over-dose increases the pain, stop it altogether. When the temporary aggravation ceases, it will be followed by an improvement.

This will cure a great number of habitual nervous head-aches, which have resisted all other treatment.

Those cases that come on with dizziness, as the first symptom, will be almost uniformly cured in this early stage by *Nux*.

In many cases of obstinate head-aches, which resist all remedies, electricity, properly applied, is a most important remedy, but it must be applied by one who understands the human system, or it may do mischief rather than good.

I have effected many permanent cures of extremely obstinate cases by this means.

I have not given directions for the use of this powerful agent, because I have been long convinced, from many examples, that it cannot be profitably or even safely used by the public, at least without some experience, and special personal instructions. Nor is it a safe agent in Allopathic hands. It is a most beautiful and beneficent Homœopathic remedy, and to be either useful or safe must be used on Homœopathic principles and in corresponding doses. I have never had the opportunity of observing its use in Allopathic hands, when it was not, like all other powerful remedies, in the same hands, as often productive of injury as benefit, and sometimes very serious injury.

INFLAMMATION OF THE EYES—OPHTHALMIA.

TREATMENT.—If this is acute, with deep redness, and severe pain, give *Acon.* and *Bell.* alternately every 2 or 3 hours till the pain is abated, and as long as it does good. At the same time, drop into the eyes, and apply over them, every 2 or 3 hours, a wash of 10 drops *Acon. tinct.* to a gill of soft water, applied as hot as can be borne. All applications to inflamed eyes, as well as to all other inflamed parts, should be warm or hot. Cold applications, though they may give momentary relief, as in burns, produce permanent reaction in the opposite direction, and do great mischief.

After the violence of the disease is abated, if there is a sore or bruised feeling of the lids, when touched, with sticking together at night, give *Hepar sul.* every 4 to 6 hours.

If the lids itch badly, with burning, *Nux.* in the same way.

In old obstinate cases, *Ars.* and *Sulph.* are required, only one at a time, 3 times a day; or, if the lids are thickened or ulcerated, *Merc.* in the same way. After the pain is abated, if redness and fulness remain, apply *Ham.*, a teaspoonfull to half a pint of water.

STYE.

Puls. or *Hepar.*, or what is generally more certain, *Apis mel.* 3 times a day. Not unfrequently one or two doses will cure a stye when taken early.

CORNS.

Shave them close, and apply a little patch of cloth on which is placed a drop of the gum from the white pine. Let it remain till it comes off of itself, when the corn will have generally disappeared; if not, apply it again. This is a sovereign remedy.

CHILBLAINS.

Ars. tinct., a teaspoonfull to a gill of water, applied affords temporary relief, but internal remedies are necessary. Of these, in ordinary cases, *Agaricus* is one of the best.

If the parts become a bluish red color, *Bell.*

If there is troublesome itching, *Nux.*, and if a few doses does not relieve, *Sulph.*

If the parts are very painful, *Phos.* Any of these may be given every 3 or 4 hours till an improvement begins.

STINGS OF INSECTS, BEES, WASPS, &c.

Ledum taken internally and applied externally is a very effectual remedy for these stings, as well as the bites of mosquitoes, flies, &c., allaying the itching and pain in a few minutes.

I am indebted to Prof. Hill for the information that a fresh onion applied to the part, is a quick and effectual remedy. If applied immediately it relieves in a few minutes. If later, it of course takes longer. A fresh piece should be applied every 10 or 15 minutes. *Am. carb.* applied to the part, and taken internally often produces the same result. Perhaps the onion is effectual from the ammonia it contains.

BITES OF RATTLESNAKES, SPIDERS, &c.

I have been for many years convinced from actual knowledge of many cases, that the most safe and effectual remedy is alcohol in any of its forms that can be most easily procured, as alcohol so much diluted as to render it tolerable, rum, whiskey, gin or brandy. It should be taken in large doses every 15 or 20 minutes till the symptoms begin to abate, or the patient feels its effects. At the same time the part bitten should be kept wet with the same. It is surprising how large a quantity will be sometimes borne in these cases. A quart or two of strong brandy has been taken in an hour or two without any other perceptible effect than to kill the poison and cure the patient. But the poison of alchol proves quite a match for Rattlesnake poison. It seems not to produce intoxication till enough has been taken to fully neutralize the poison, and the excess only produces the ordinary effects.

MECHANICAL INJURIES, BLOWS, FALLS, BRUISES, SPRAINS, &c.

Arnica is the great remedy in these accidents. It should be taken internally in pellets and the parts injured rubbed frequently or kept wet with *Arn. tint.*, a teaspoonfull in half a pint of water. If inflammation and fever follow, give *Acon.*

But where the skin is broken, or the flesh torn, *Calendula* is the remedy used externally the same as *Arn.* It acts like magic in allaying pain and preventing inflammation. The edges of the cut or torn wounds should, of course, be brought as near together as possible, and kept there.

FATIGUE.

When the muscles become fatigued by long walking or excessive labor or over exertion, a few doses, or even a single dose of *Arn.* or *Rhus.* affords great relief. If particular mucles or limbs are sore and lame, rub them with the *Arn.* wash.

BURNS AND SCALDS.

Apply, as quickly as possible, alcohol, whisky, rum, brandy, spirits of turpentine or soft soap, and keep it on, and the part thoroughly protected from the air till pain subsides. Nothing is better than soft soap, and this is generally at hand. I have seen this applied from my early boyhood, and have never seen any thing do better. Cold water, though it feels comfortable for the moment, it is a very bad application. The above treatment cures burns in half the time. If there is fever, give *Acon.*

CARBUNCLE.

This appears, at first, much like a common boil, but larger and much more painful, and with much more constitutional disorder. It does not come to a point like a boil, but is broad and flat on the top with several openings instead of one. It is attended with chill, loss of appetite, depression of spirits, fever and prostration.

It more commonly appears on the back, or the neck. It is attended with great destruction of the flesh, which mortifies and falls out, leaving a large cavity which is very slow in healing. At the close, the patient is as much reduced as after a long fever.

Treatment.—Give, in the beginning, *Ammon carb.* 3 grains in a gill of water, teaspoonfull doses every 2 hours, and apply a cloth wet in the same, but twice as strong and hot, to the part—continue it as long as it does good. If it goes on, and openings appear in it, and the pain is not abated, stop this and give *Ars.* every 2 or 3 hours. At the same time apply *caustic* potash powdered, in and around the openings, so that, as it dissolves, it will run into the openings, and penetrate as deep as possible into the heart of the tumour. Apply this once daily, placing over it a warm, soft poultice of slippery elm, flax seed or bread. The above treatment is much better and more successful than that ordinarily practiced. The application of the caustic speedily changes and relieves the terrible burning pain of the carbuncle, and the *Ars.* aids in this, and preserves the system from running down, and greatly shortens the disease. Carbuncle should never be laid open by the knife.

MALIGNANT PUSTULE.

This affection is of frequent occurence during some seasons, though its name is not generally known. A large number of cases have occurred during the last year. It was, for a long time, not distinguished from the carbuncle, which it considerably resembles, though essentially different. It is much smaller, and is generally located on the extremities.

It seems, at first, like the bite of some insect, and the patient generally thinks it is. It is, at first, a little, red, somewhat pointed elevation like a small boil, with the appearance of a little hole in the tip. It is painful and burning. The inflammation increases rapidly and runs up the limb. If it occurs on the toe, for example—the whole top of the foot becomes rapidly red and swollen.

If it goes on, it soon has several openings in it like a carbuncle, and ends in suppuration and destruction of the substance, leaving a large opening. It is attended with pretty severe, generally burning, pain, and considerable feverish disturbance.

TREATMENT.—*Ammon carb.* is the specific and effectual remedy, given as in carbuncle, and applied in the same way. The pain is often relieved in 15 minutes, and in 24 hours the whole character of the disease is changed, and the inflammation subdued. Since using this remedy, we have not found occasion for any other.

FELON—WHITLOW.

This comes on with a pricking, sharp pain, inducing the belief that there is a splinter or brier in the finger.

TREATMENT.—When first felt, put the whole hand in cold water—the colder the better—until it becomes benumed, then wrap it in flannel till it becomes thoroughly warmed. If there is still pain, repeat the process till the pain ceases. This course will either cure the disease altogether, or render it a comparatively painless one.

DISEASES OF WOMEN AND CHILDREN—FIRST OF WOMEN.

Amenorrhœa-Absence of the Monthly Turns.

When a stoppage or suppression occurs in young girls, *Puls.* 3 times a day, or *Cauloph.*, or *Mac.*, the two last alternately. If the menses do not make their appearance at the usual age, if the health does not suffer, do nothing. In no case give what are called "forcing medicines." They do great mischief, and are often dangerous, and are the source of long-lasting difficulties.

If sudden suppression is produced by a chill, or getting wet, put the patient in bed, give one or more doses of *Gels.*, put the feet in hot water, apply hot wet cloths to the lower part of the abdomen, or use, if convenient, the warm sitz bath. If not soon relieved, give *Puls.*

If the suppression is produced by a fright, give one or more doses of *Acon.*, then *Puls.*

If, at the time when the menses should come on, there are nervous or hysterical symptoms or spasms, *Cocculus* every hour or two.

If there is Leucorrhœa or Whites, instead of the regular menses, *Cauloph.*, *Mac.*, *Puls.*, and *Sepia* are the remedies—either one alone, or either two alternately, 3 or 4 times a day.

If suppression has been of long standing in girls, with paleness, weakness, palpitation of the heart, &c., the remedies are *Calc. carb.*, *Ferrum*, *Puls.*, *Sepia.*, and *Sulph.* Either of these may be taken 3 times a day for a week, when, if not improved, take another in the same manner.

Dysmenorrhœa—Painful Menstruation.

If the flow is profuse, with pain and sickness of the stomach, give *Ipecac* every half hour till relieved. *Mac.* or *Cauloph.* may be used in the same way—the first, especially, if there is head-ache.

If there are spasms in the abdomen, hysterical symptoms, difficulty of breathing, and especially if the discharge is black, *Coc.*

But *Cauloph.*, *Mac.*, and *Puls.*, are, in general, the three most important remedies. When there are no particular reasons for using other remedies, the patient may take either of them, (perhaps usually *Cauloph.* is the best), or either two of them alternately, every 15 or 20 minutes till the severe pain is relieved.

During the interval of a month, a dose of *Cauloph.* one day, and *Mac.* the next, will generally prevent these painful recurrences, and effect a permanent cure. But there are obstinate cases of this painful difficulty, depending on particular causes, which cannot be prescribed for without personal attention.

Profuse Menstruation—Flowing.

If this is attended with pressing down pains, and pain in the back, *Bell.* every half hour, till this is relieved. If much reduced by loss of blood, a few doses of *China.* But the most important remedy is *Hamamelis.* If at all urgent, a drop of the tincture may be given every half hour, and if at all alarming, injections into the womb with a female syringe, if at hand, if not, with any other, of a teaspoonfull of the tincture in a gill of cold water, and often repeated if necessary. This is equally appropriate whether the flowing occurs at the monthly period, or any other. All this is for present relief. But for those who have, habitually too frequent and too profuse menstruation, and who are at the same time, somewhat feeble, give, during the interval, *Nux.* every night, and *China* every morning, for two weeks, and during the remainder of the interval, *Calc. carb.*

one night, and *Sulph.* the next. This will seldom fail to bring about an improvement, but if the state is not entirely corrected, repeat the same during the next interval. This has cured many cases of long standing in one, two or three months, which had been treated for years without benefit.

The worst cases of flowing after delivery, are speedily checked by copious injections of cold water with *Hamamelis* or *Arn.* and drop doses of *Hamam.* The cold water injections, so much feared by some at such times, are perfectly safe. I have used them hundreds of times, and for many years, and never had reason to regret their use.

Leucorrhœa—Whites.

This diseased condition, so common among feeble women, is seldom permanently cured by the old drugging process, astringents, &c., but the most stubborn cases are daily cured by skillful Homœopathic treatment. There are cases attended with ulcerations, and other diseased conditions, which require the personal attentions of the physician; but by following the brief directions which follow, a great majority of the cases will be cured more promptly than is done by the ordinary prevalent medical treatment.

The remedies generally required in domestic practice are *Caul.*, *Mac.*, *Pod.* and *Puls.* In most cases the two first are sufficient. One may be taken every morning, and the other every evneing, in a dose of one two grains. Hundreds of cases will be cured by these two remedies.

If the disease has continued for some time, it is frequently attended by a bearing down, prolapsus or falling of the womb. This will disappear with the curing of the Leucorrhœa.

Pod. is specially appropriate where bearing down, and Leucorrhœa come on after confinement—a grain 3 times a day.

If Leucorrhœa accompanies suppression of the menses, *Puls.* is the efficient remedy, 3 or 4 times daily.

When the discharge is acrid or irritating, or there is internal smarting or burning, injections of the *Hydrastis* wash as prepared for scarlet fever is often extremely useful.

A dependence on mechanical supports for the cure of prolapsus is productive of infinite mischief. If the discharge is like jelly, or if it produces itching or burning, *Sepia* 3 or 4 times a day.

Sickness and Vomiting During Pregnancy.

This is sometimes a very troublesome and even dangerous affection, but by Homœopathic treatment can almost uniformly be promptly relieved. For this we have many remedies, and it is well to know several, as sometimes one agrees best, and sometimes another. Often a remedy gives prompt relief, but soon loses its influence, and another will be equally prompt. The patient may have a choice of the following:

Merc., in a majority of cases, is a sufficient remedy.

If not, *Ipecac, Arsenicum, Nux., Puls., Sepia., Pod., Tart. and Verat.* may be employed, each with good effect in different cases. They may be taken from once to five or six times a day, according to necessity. A dose of *Mac.* at night, or *Ipecac,* &c., will often prevent the usual sickness in the morning.

Confinement—Child-bed Difficulties.

As a preparation for labor, a multitude of observing Homœopathic physicians now testify to the great benefit of *Mac.* and *Caul.* They render the labor much shorter, and much easier, and prevent after pains. Many who have always had tedious and difficult labors have quick and easy ones after this preparation. A grain of one may be taken at night, and a grain of the other in the morning for some weeks before confinement. These two remedies have proved a blessing to thousands.

Irregular and Ineffectual Labor Pains.

Caul., one grain every quarter or half hour till the pains become regular, which will generally be after one or two doses. *Bell.* and *Nux.* are often effectual remedies. In tedious labors, from a rigid and unyielding state of the parts, *Gels.*, in doses of 3 drops, acts like a charm.

After-Pains.

Caul. is the potent remedy, unless their is excessive flowing, notwithstanding its use, when injections of cold water with tinct. of *Hamam.*, are required.

Inflammation and Swelling of the Breasts.

Early in the attack, if it comes on with a chill, a few doses of *Gels.*, as in fever, by producing perspiration, dissipates the disease. But if this does not check the inflammation, give *Acon.* and *Bell.* alternately every 2 hours till the inflammation is somewhat abated, and then *Bry.* and *Bell.* Keep the breasts covered with a cloth wrung out of warm water.

But if the case has been neglected, or badly treated, till the suppuration has taken place, and the breast is discharging, give *Phos.* 3 times a day. If it has been of long standing, and the breast is very hard after the discharge has continued for some time, *Calc. carb.*, *Silicia* or *Sulph.*, may be required.

Sore Nipples.

Apply frequently a wash of *Hydrastis*—10 drops to a table spoonfull of water. Or if the nipple is raw, *Calend.*

Milk-Leg.

Under the ordinary treatment, this is a most severe and protracted disease. The old school have never learned to *cure* it. The following directions will enable a husband to treat his wife for this serious affection, with vastly greater success, and cure her in one quarter the time that is required by Allopathic treatment, in the hands of the most skillful physicians.

It generally makes its attacks within one or two weeks after confinement, like most other inflammatory diseases, with chilliness and fever. Pain usually com mences in the loins, back and lower part of the bowels, extending to the groin, and thence down the limb. This commences to swell, and in two days the whole limb may be twice its natural size. Though hot and inflamed, it is not red, but of a very marked white. The feeling is hard and elastic. The disease consists of inflammation of the veins, and along the principal veins down the inside of the thigh, and back of the leg is the principal pain. These veins may be traced with the finger, enlarged and hard like a cord, and very tender. These lines are interrupted now and then by a hard knob. Under the usual treatment, the limb does not return to its natural state and size for a long time, often for years—sometimes never. It is not unfrequently followed by a dropsical state.

TREATMENT.—As soon as this affection is ascertained, give *Hamamelis tinct.*, 10 drops in a tumbler of water —teaspoonfull doses every 2 or 3 hours.

Rub the limb faithfully with a wash of the same— 2 teaspoonsfull to a gill of water, applied as warm as possible. When the pain and tenderness are considerably abated, give the remedy less frequently, and apply it chiefly along the line of the hard and tender veins on the inside of the thigh, and back of the leg, by rubbing and wet cloths. Continue this treatment less and less vigorously till the soreness and pain have entirely disappeared, and rub the limb with the wash daily, till the swelling subsides. If, after this, any considerable weakness is felt, give *Nux.* at night, and *Ars.* in the morning. Under this treatment, this formidable and dreaded disease will be comparatively trifling. Dropsy will not follow this treatment. When it follows the old routine, it requires skillful treatment.

GENERAL DIRECTIONS.

Never give physic after confinement. It is productive of infinite mischief. If the bowels are not moved in 2 or 3 days, give *Nux.* at night, and *Bry.* in the morning. If delayed 4 or 5 days, give injections of warm water This is always sufficient, and avoids the long train of evils that follow the use of cathartics.

The proper treatment of a woman, after confinement, is as follows: After resting for a few minutes, inject into the womb a pint of cool water, containing a few drops of *Arn.* or *Calendula* tinct. If the flowing is excessive, repeat it with *Hamamelis.* Apply cloths wrung out of cool water, to the parts, instead of hot and dry ones. Wash the patient all over with a wet cloth or sponge of a temperature to suit the feelings of the patient, without too much exposure of the surface, and carefully avoiding any chilliness. After washing and rubbing dry, put a wet bandage around her, instead of a dry one, covered with a flannel or cotton one, dry. Keep the room thoroughly aired and cool. Repeat the washing daily. Be no more afraid of water and air, than before confinement. Under this treatment, a woman will be as well and as strong at the end of 4 or

5 days, as in 2 or 3 weeks under the old abominable, physicing, confining and heating treatment. I am perfectly aware that many, both in and out of the professsion, are horrified at this dreadful exposure at such a time. They seem to labor not only under a hydrophobia, but an airphobia. They relate cases in which women, after confinement, have been thrown into fevers, and had broken breasts, and even died from merely touching their hands to a cold wet cloth. This all may very well be. Shut a woman up in a tight, hot room, and roast her for several days without a breath of fresh air, *before* confinement, or *after*, and she will take cold by a very slight exposure, and so will a man. But let a woman go on after confinement with the same free use of both air and water, to which she has previously been accustomed, and she is in no danger of taking cold, unless the exposure is so great as to produce chilliness.

The advantages of the cold injections are the following:

1st. The internal organs, after labor, are hot, fatigued and exhausted. An application of cool water to them is always extremely greatful to the feeling of the patient, quieting and strengthening.

2d. It produces an immediate and prompt contraction of the womb, and thus insures the patient against an unnecessary or dangerous loss of blood, by flowing.

3d. It is a sovereign preventive of atter-pains, which often produce so much suffering and exhaustion.

This will be plain when it is understood how after-pains are produced. When the womb is not well contracted, but remains open, blood flows into it, and coagulates until it becomes accumulated in such a quantity, that it excites the womb to contract, in order to expel it, just as it contracted to expel the child, and after-birth. The pains come on just as often as there is a sufficient accumulation of coagulated blood to render them necessary to remove it, and no oftener. But if the womb is made to contract vigorously at first, by cool water injection, no such accumulation can take place, and there is no occasion for pains to expel it, and of course there are no pains. Why do after-pains increase with every successive confinement, so that after a woman has had many children, they often become even more distressing, than the labor itself?

It is simply because the womb becomes so much distended and weakened, that it does not contract promptly after delivery, but remains open so that blood flows into it, in large quantities, causing repeated efforts to expel it, and each effort produces an after-pain. A few injections of cool water, or cold if necessary, immediately, by giving tone to the weakened organ, produces the same prompt contraction that took place spontaneously in early labors, and of course, the same freedom from after-pains. I have witnessed the delightful results of this treatment for years, and in hundreds of cases. Many patients who had the greatest fears of it at first are now loudest in its praise.

Hydropathic practitioners have long practiced it, and

hundreds of other physicians, witnessing its safety and success, have adopted it, and *all* are delighted with it. I have received every year, from succesive classes of medical students in the medical college, to whom I have taught the uses of water and air, numerous letters, thanking me for the teaching and speaking in rapturous terms of the success of the practice and the reputation they have gained by it. I have never yet known of the first case of mischief done by it, when administered with any sort of prudence. The old ruinous, roasting and physicking practice is fast going out of fashion and common sense taking its place.

The woman, after confinement, should abstain from all stimulating drinks and have only light, unstimulating food till after the milk is fully established. If the after-pains require it, give *Caul.* By this course, the milk fever on the second or third day, so common within my recollection, with often a broken breast in its train, will be avoided. A woman with a good physician and a good nurse should have neither milk fever or a broken breast.

Nursing Sore Mouth.

This is a sore mouth mostly affecting nursing women, but sometimes coming on some weeks before confinement. Under the old treatment it is a very troublesome and often an incorrigible disease. If it continues for some time, it frequently extends along the mucous membrane of the stomach and bowels, producing intolerance of food and an obstinate diarrhea, under which the patient is rapidly exhausted. Many mothers are obliged to wean the child before the disease can be cured.

By a very simple Homœopathic treatment, it is almost invariably and rapidly cured.

Treatment.—*Pod.*, 3 grains in a tumbler of water, a teaspoonfull before each meal and at bed-time, if begun in an early stage, often effects a speedy cure. If the case is not improving in a few days, take *Nux.* every night and *Ars.* every morning. I have cured cases with these two remedies in a week or ten days that had been six or eight months under treatment without benefit.

Hydrastis is, in many cases, an invaluable remedy every 3 to 6 hours. It may be made of the strength of 6 or 8 drops to a tumbler of water and taken in teaspoonfull doses—the mouth being well washed with the same before each dose, or the wash may be made two or three times as strong.

In cases of long standing, where the bowels have become affected and the above treatment is not successful after a reasonable trial, *Pod.* and *Leptand.* are invaluable. One may be taken at a time or the two alternated every 3 to 6 hours—2 or 3 grains in half a tumbler of water and teaspoonfull doses.

There is not one case of nursing sore mouth in a hundred that will not be cured by this treatment, and in a much shorter time than it is usually done under medical supervision.

In a few obstinate cases in diseased constitutions, it may be necessary to take *Sulph.*, 2 doses daily, for a few days, or *Sulph.* and *Calc. carb.*

Nervousness.

Many women, as well as some men, in bad health, have a train of symptoms well known as nervous. These symptoms generally depend upon a diseased or disordered state of some organ or organs, of which this nervous condition is only a symptom, and which must be cured in order to remove this symptom. But these distressing nervous sensations may often be greatly alleviated by palliative remedies. One of the most generally useful is *Ambra grisia.* In almost any condition attended with nervous restlessness and sleeplessness, if not in an acute fever or inflammation, an occasional dose of *Ambra* will allay the irritability and procure sleep, without any of the disagreeble consequences of opiates.

Almost all nervous affections of long standing depend upon some *other* chronic diseased condition which must be the chief object of attention. Most of these cases require the judicious application of electricity. Cases of "broken down" nervous conditions of women, of many years standing, I have often restored to comfortable health and enjoyment by this beautiful agent with other appropriate Homœopathic treatment.

Electricity is a strictly Homœopathic remedy, and when used on Homœopathic principles, is a most effectual agent in a long catalogue of diseases of a chronic character, that is, of long standing—indeed to almost every disease after it has become chronic, and in which long diseased parts require to have their exhausted vitality restored. But administered on Allopathic principles and in Allopathic quantity, it is capable of doing, and often does, serious mischief, exhausting, instead of restoring vitality.

Among the chronic diseases in which electricity has been, and is daily being, of the greatest utility, a cure being often rapidly effected after the failure of all other means, are rheumatism, neuralgia, palsy, asthma, dyspepsia, affections of the head, head-ache, tendency to insanity, liver affections, old ulcers, all chronic inflammations, affections of the kidneys, enlarged and relaxed abdomen in women who have borne many children with falling of the bowels, prolapsus uteri, and leucorrhea, tendency to dropsy, &c., &c. Many of these cases will be permanently cured by the aid of electricity which cannot be cured without. I have very lately greatly relieved a case of asthma of 6 years standing which had resisted all other treatment, by a single application.

DISEASES OF CHILDREN.

Sore Mouths of Infants.

Touch the mouth all over the sore surface, not rub it, with a wash of *Hydras.* of the strength of 10 drops to a table-spoonful of water, 3 or 4 times a day. The child will swallow a sufficient quantity for a dose each time it is used. *Merc.*, *Nux.*, *Cham.* and *Sulph.* acid are also effectual remedies. Either of them may be given 3 or 4 times a day.

Stoppage of the Nose—" Snuffles."

Nux. is the sufficient remedy. Besides giving it internally 3 or 4 times a day, a prompt method of relief is, to rub up a few pellets very fine with a little sugar, and blow a few grains up the nostrils through a quill.

Crying.

When infants cry, it is always for some good reason. Endeavor carefully to ascertain the cause. It may be an uncomfortable state of the dress; it may be chafed, and the sore parts are rendered painful by being suffered to remain wet. It may be ear-ache, or more probably colic. If it is chafed, keep the parts dry—give *Cham.* 3 times a day and wash the parts as often with *Hydras.* as for sore mouth or Calendula. If not soon better, give *Sulph.* twice a day. If it proceeds from ear-ache, the child will manifest it by uneasy movements of the head, and often by screams. In this case, if there is fever, give *Acon.* and *Bell.* every 2 hours till the fever subsides, then *Bell.* alone. If this fails after a few doses, give *Cham.* and *Puls.* If the crying arises from colic, give *Cham.*, *Coloc.*, or *Bell.*

A great deal of colicky pain and crying are caused by feeding the child when it should not be fed. It is a mistaken and very mischievous notion, that a child must have food within a few hours after birth. If this were so, an all-wise Creator who makes all necessary provisions for his creatures, would have provided it. The bare fact that the mother does not usually have milk for it before the second or third day, is sufficient proof that the child does not need it before that time. For at least 36 hours it should not be fed at all unless the mother furnishes food before. A teaspoonfull of water occasionally is the only thing it should swallow.

Above all, avoid medicine of every description, even catnip or saffron tea. Some seem to suppose that every child is both sick and starving as soon as it draws its first breath, and it must be outraged by unnatural food and more unnatural medicine. Nine-tenths of all the fits, the vomiting, the colic and the crying in young children are produced by this abominable and unnatural treatment. Dr. Dewes, whose experience is very great, says he has never known a young infant have fits that had not been fed or dosed.

If the mother's milk, from any cause, is delayed longer than 36 hours, the child may be cautiously fed with a mixture of new thin cream, from milk that has stood not more than two or three hours, and water, with the slightest perceptible taste of pure white sugar, the proportion being 3 parts water to 1 of cream.

Scald-Head.—Milk Crusts.

When sores first come upon a child's head, discharging a fluid and forming scabs, *Rhus.* is the first remedy, three times a day for at least a week or two, and longer if the disease is improving. If it fails to effect a cure, sulphur 3 times a day; if the eruption is dry and scurvy, *Ars.* Wash the head clean daily with soap and water. In a majority of cases, however, *Dulcamara*, 3 times a day, is the only necessary remedy.

Itch, whether in Children or Adults.

Croton. tig. and *Lobel.* alternately every 6 or 8 hours will generally moderate the itching in a single day, and, as I know from experience, cure the disease in a week or two. If it fails after this length of time or is not improving, give *Merc. cor.* three times a day for a week, and then the first remedies as before. Drying up the disease suddenly by external applications, is a dangerous practice, often producing a variety of internal disorders, and sometimes death.

If the disease is incorrigible, however, there is no danger in a weak sulphur ointment, (1 part of sulphur to 10 of lard) thoroughly rubbed into the sores, at the same time that sulphur in Homœopathic doses, is taken internally three times a day.

Croton. is a valuable remedy in a variety of eruptions attended by troublesome itching, and so is *Lobelia,* in those eruptions that resemble the itch in appearance.

"Summer Complaints."

There are two distinct diseases that go by this name, viz: Cholera Infantum and Diarrhœa. The most obvious distinction between them is, that the first is attended with vomiting and the latter is not.

Cholera Infantum.

This is a very prevalent and very fatal disease in this country, especially in cities. It chiefly affects children between the ages of three months and three years. It sometimes comes on with vomiting and diarrhœa at the same time, but quite as often the vomiting does not come on till the diarrhœa has contiuued for a few hours, or a day or two. It is often rapid in its progress, and fatal in two or three days. At other times it is of long continuance, and reduces the little sufferer to a skeleton. It is attended with considerable fever, coated or red tongue, quick pulse, a good deal of pain and suffering, great restlessness and rapid failure of strength. The child sleeps with the eyes partly open. The evacuations are frequent and exceedingly various in appearance, being yellow, brown or green—often grass-green or mixed, and sometimes the color often changing, scarcely any two successive evacuations being alike. In this disease, there is always inflammation of the mucous membrane of the stomach, or bowels, or both, and inflammation or congestion of the liver. According as the stomach or bowels are most affected, the vomiting or diarrhœa will predominate. If the disease goes on for some time, the brain is apt to become sympathetically affected, and under the Allopathic treatment of opiates, hopelessly diseased.

TREATMENT.—In the early state of the vomiting and diarrhœa, give *Ipecac* after every act of vomiting or purging. This alone is often sufficient to arrest the disease. If it fails, and especially, if there is thirst, give *Ars.* in the same manner, not more than four pellets in half a tumbler of water, teaspoonfull doses. If there is great restlessness, *Cham.* alternated with either of the above remedies.

If the evacuations are yellow, brown, or dark, *Pod.* is an effectual remedy; 2 grains in half a tumbler of water, a teaspoonfull same as the other remedies. When the evacuations are green, *Agaricus* is the best remedy, or *Cham.*, *Merc. sol.* or *Pod.*

If the patient is much reduced, and the vomiting and diarrhœa continue, *Ars.* and *Verat.*

In many obstinate and protracted cases, when there is reason to believe that the bowels are ulcerated, *Hydras.* will save the patient.

Pod., in alternation with either of the above two remedies, is also applicable in the same case.

Diarrhœa.

Occurring in hot weather, or from indigestion, is usually quickly arrested by *Ipecac* or *Nux.*, or both alternated. If the evacuations are thin and watery, *Ars.* alone, or with *Verat.*

If they are green, *Agaricus* or *Cham.* or both. If they are yellow, brown or dark, *Pod.*

If the disease has been of long standing, *Pod.* and *Lept.* or *Hydrast.* will often effect cures in cases that seem very discouraging. The remedy should be repeated after each evacuation.

There are no diseases which require greater caution in diet than Cholera Infantum and Diarrhæa. When cases are almost cured, the least imprudence in diet will cause a relapse which may be fatal. *Dulc.* is sufficient in a great many cases of Diarrhœa, especialy in damp weather.

Incontinence of Urine—Wetting the Bed.

The principal remedies are *Apis. mel.*, *Canth.* and *Pod.* One of them may be given three or four times a day. *Phos.* acid is often effectual.

Convulsions—Spasms—Fits.

These are frequently produced by indigestible food or excess, as from raisins, nuts, pastry, &c. In these cases, if it can be done, get down a sufficient quantity of warm water to produce vomiting. Whether this is effected or not, give *Nux.*, two or three doses every 2 or 3 hours.

If from worms, give *Santonine*, as directed under that head. If from a nervous condition, without the above obvious causes, *Bell.*, *Cham.*, *Amb.*, *Nux.* or *Ignatia.*

During the fit, put the child in a cold bath, and apply a cloth wet in cold water to the head, then wrap in warm flannels and get the patient warm as soon as possible.

Weakness of the Limbs—Slowness in learning to Walk.

Calc. carb. 2 or 3 pellets every day for a week, then *Sulph.* in the same way. After stopping a week, if necessary repeat it. An improvement will soon be apparent.

Croup.

Give *Acon.* and *Spongia* every 10, 15 or 20 minutes if the case is urgent, if not, less frequently.

If not relieved by a few doses, give *Sulph.* acid every hour till there is an improvement, then less often.—*Hepar* is often an effectual remedy.

At the beginning, put a cloth wrung out of cold water over the throat and chest, and cover it well with a flannel, renewed every hour.

Hooping Cough.

Corallium rubrum and *Chelidonium* often cure this disease like a charm, and these may be first tried alternately every 2, 3 or 4 hours, according to the frequency of the cough; or during the early stage; while there is a fever, give *Acon.* or *Gels.* and *Ipecac* or *Nux.* every three or four hours. In a latter stage, when the fever has subsided, *Bell.* and *Verat.*, or *Bell.* and *Merc. sol.*

Falling or Protrusion of the Bowels.

Nux. and *Ignatia* are the best remedies, but only one at a time, three or four times a day.

Teething.

The process of cutting teeth often produces great disturbance in the infantile organism. The child is feverish, and often exceedingly peevish and irritable. *Acon.* and *Gels.* are effective remedies while there is a feverish state, repeated as often as required. If there is no fever, *Ambra* or *Coffea*.

INDEX.

www.ingramcontent.com/pod-product-compliance
Lightning Source LLC
LaVergne TN
LVHW011120110826
845150LV00008B/2204
* 9 7 8 1 4 2 5 5 0 4 4 2 7 *